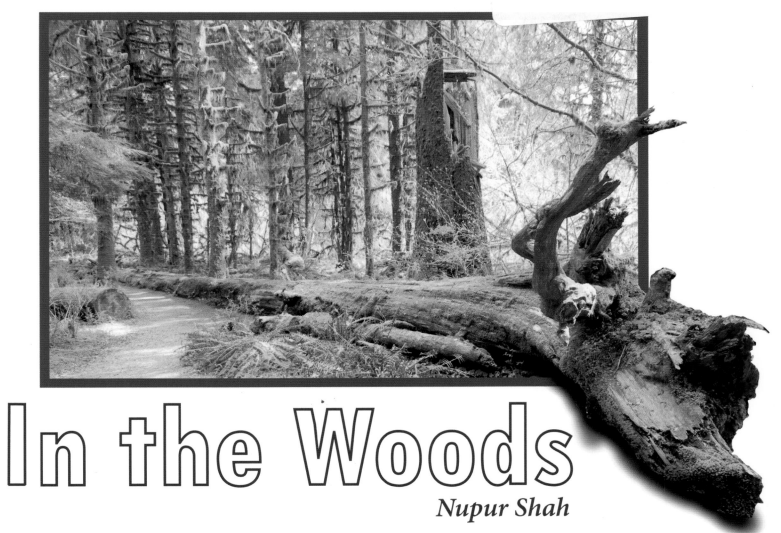

In the Woods

Nupur Shah

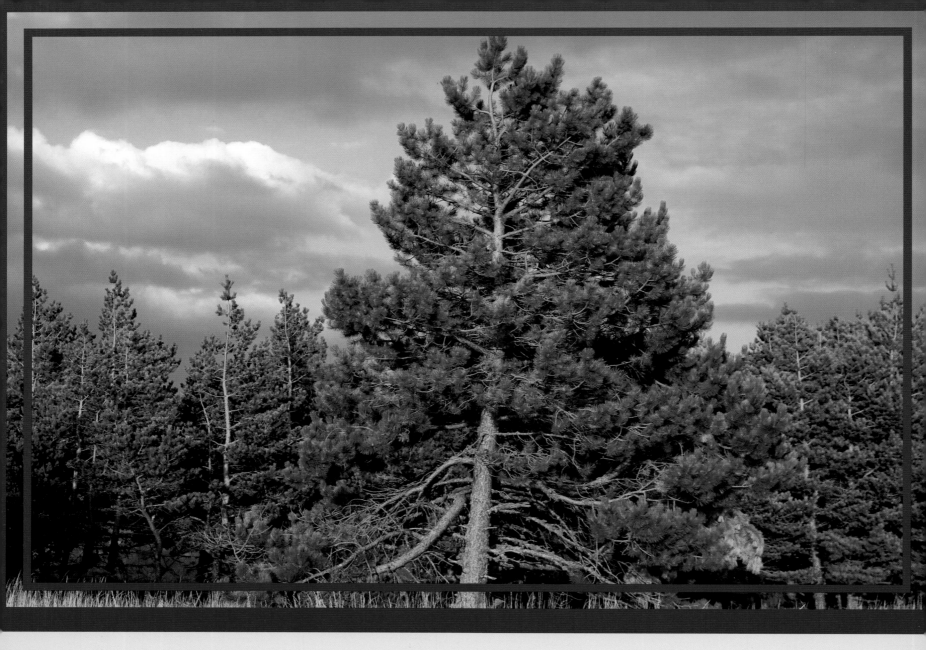

 Here is a tree.

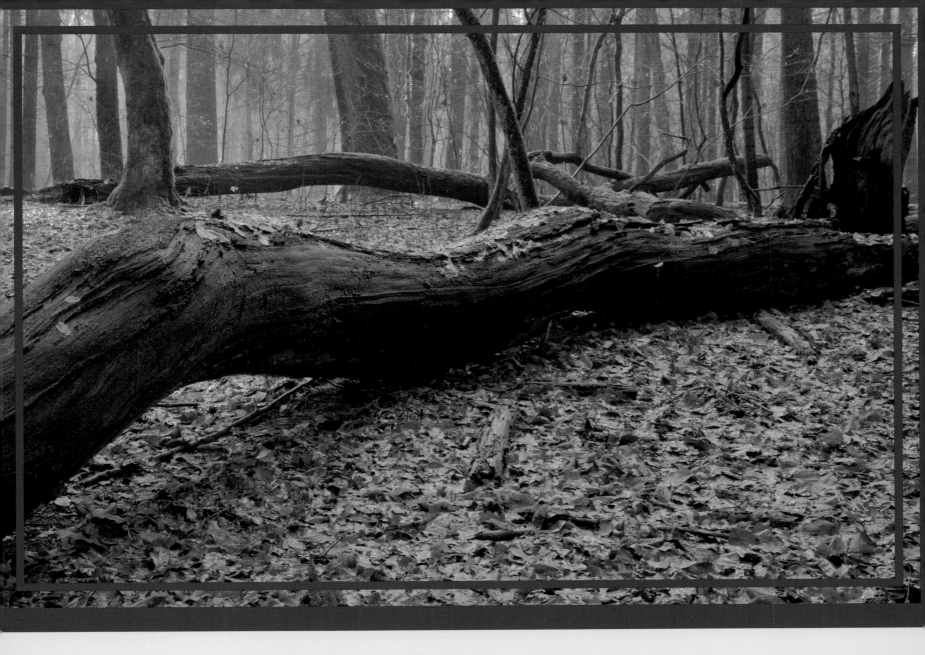

Here is a log.

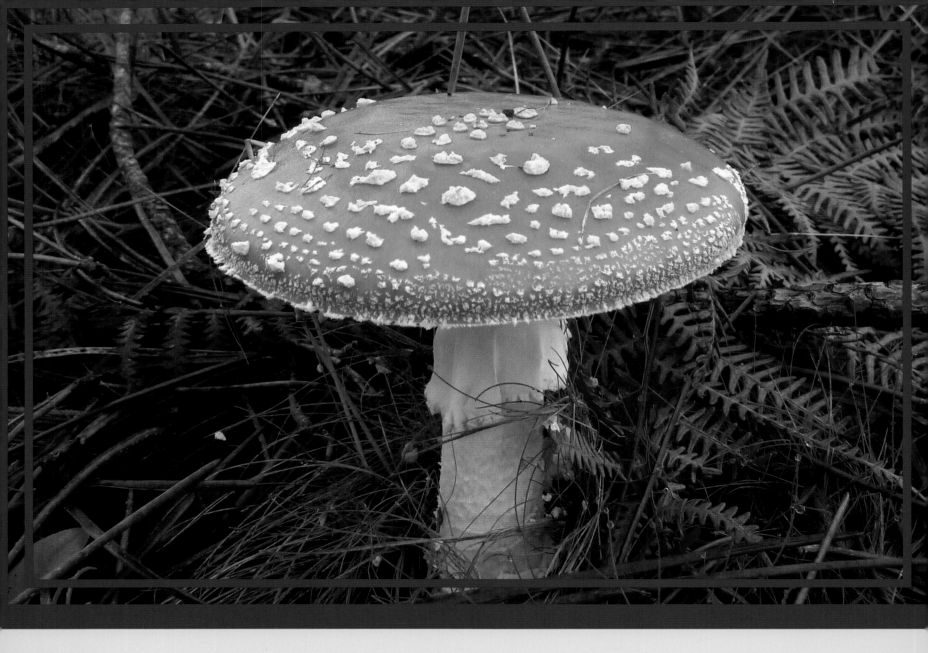

 4 Here is a mushroom.

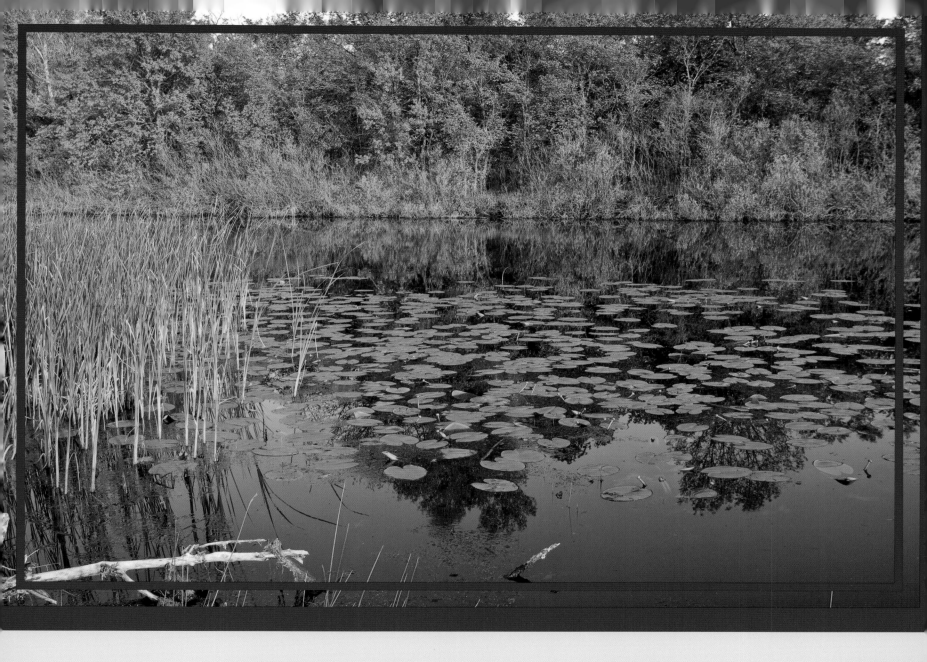

Here is a pond.

5

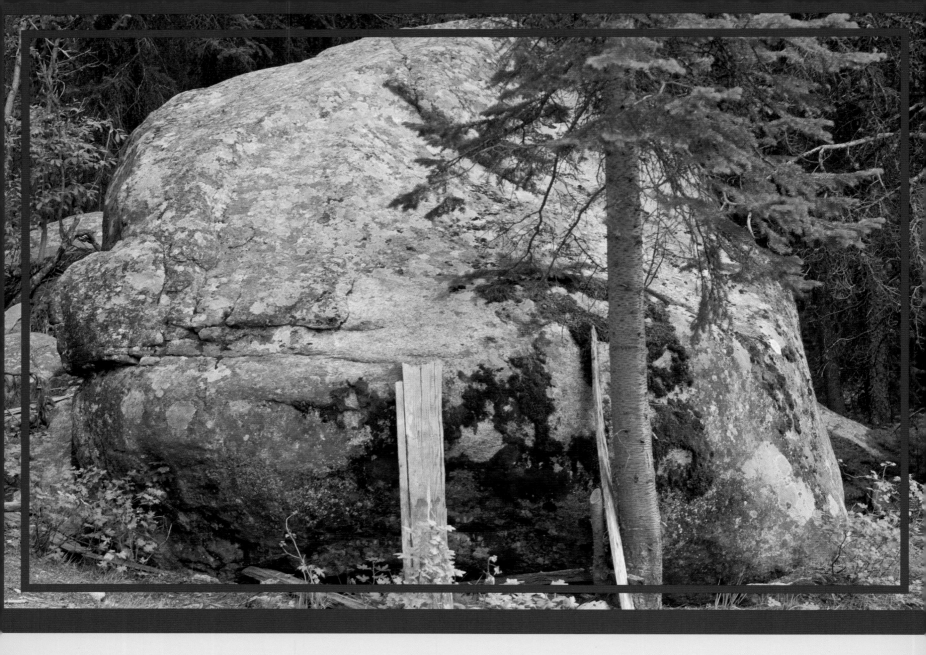

 6

Here is a rock.

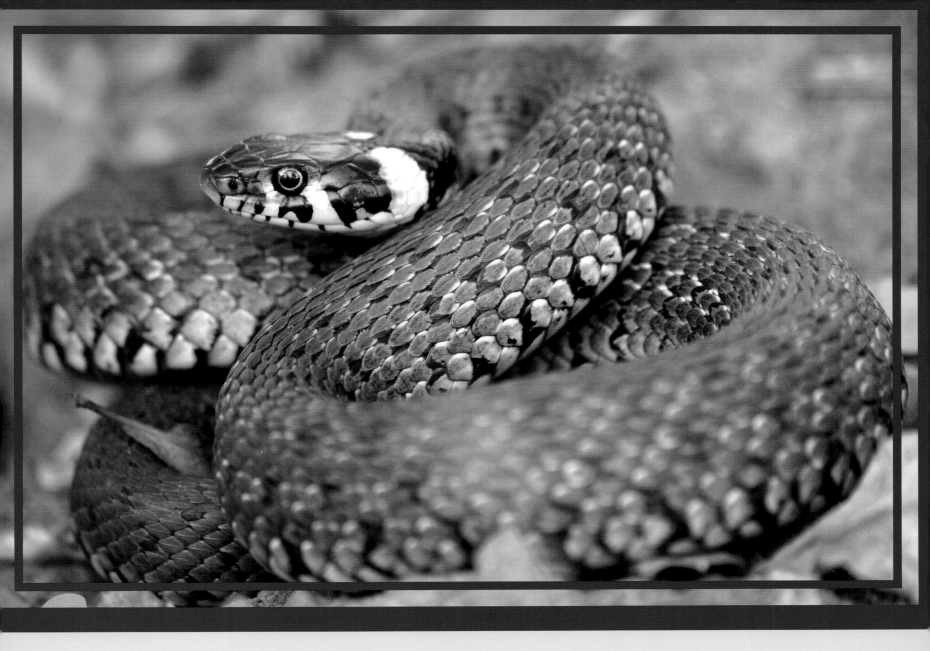

Here is a snake.

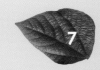

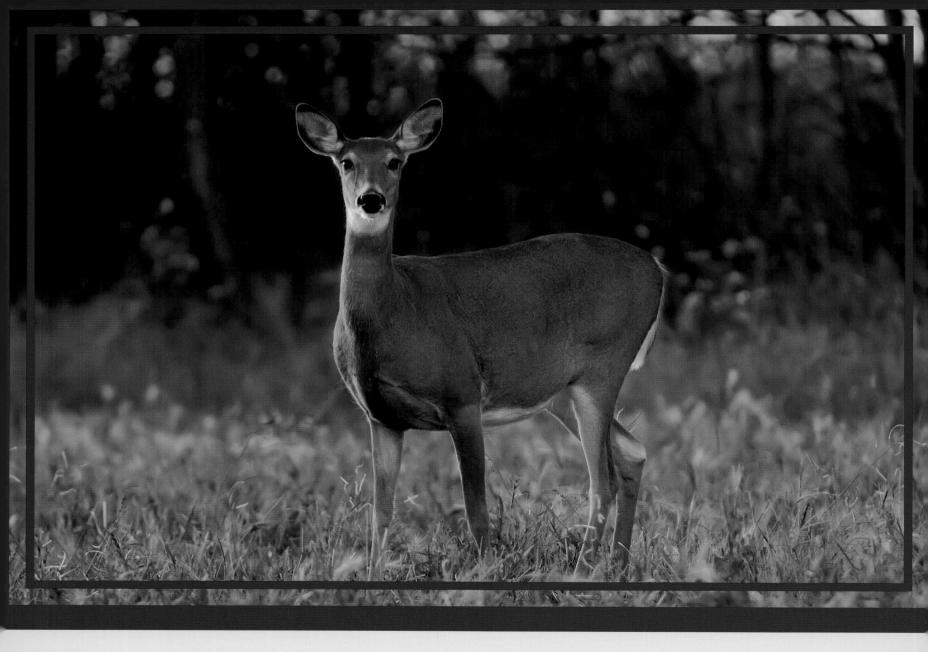

Here is a deer.

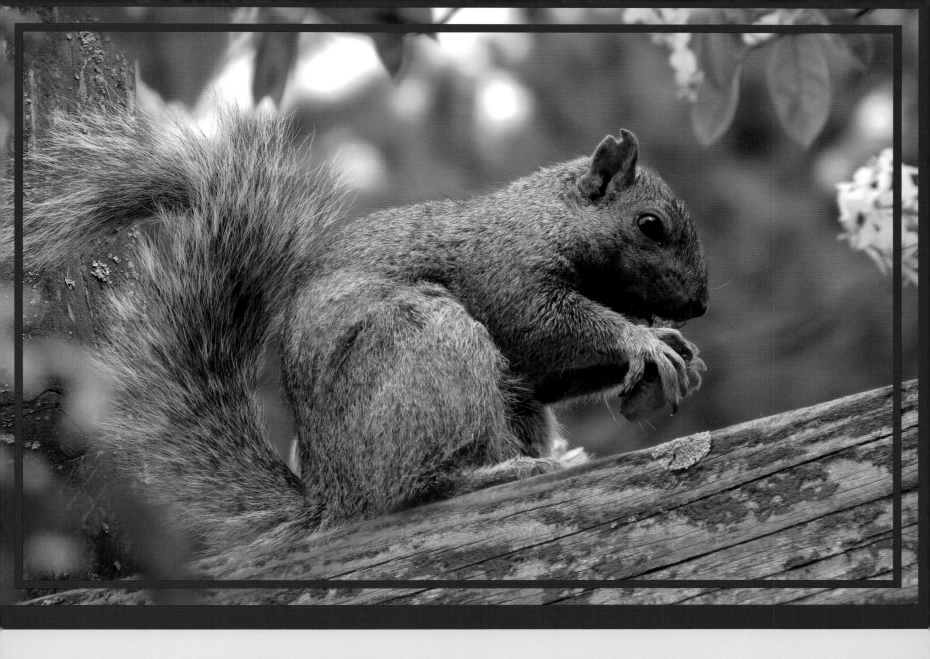

Here is a squirrel.

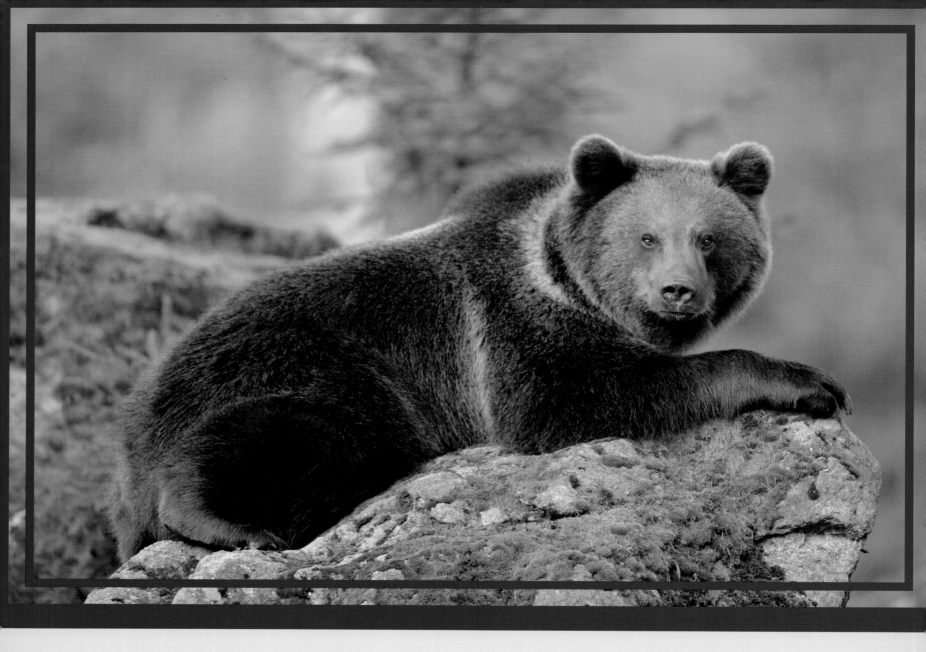

10

Here is a bear.

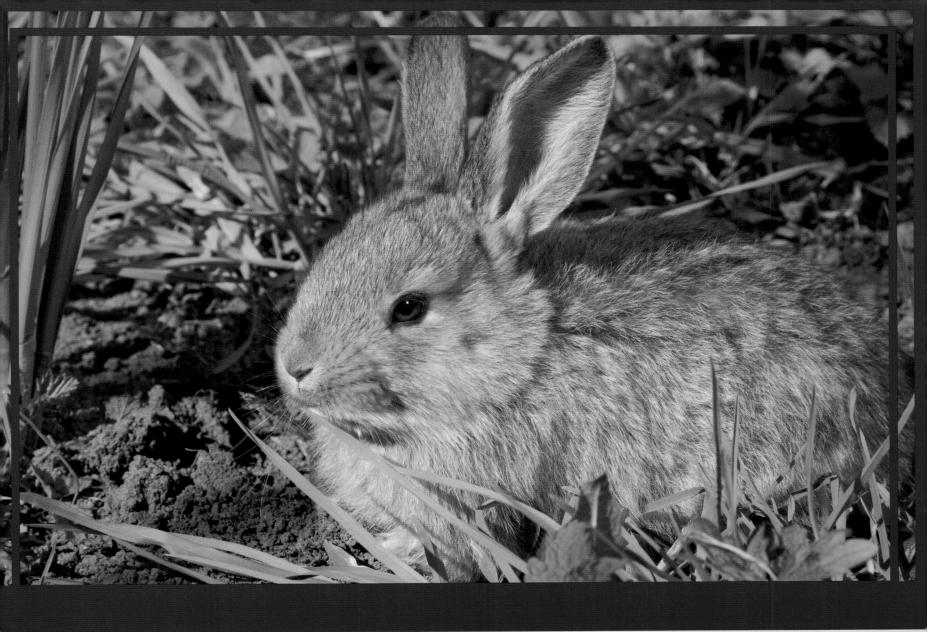

Here is a rabbit.

Power Words
How many can you read?

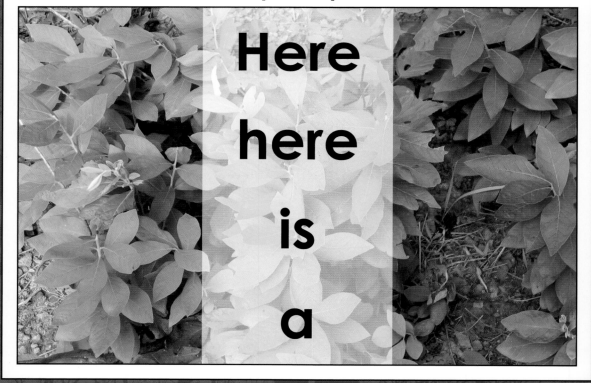

Here

here

is

a